The Penguin

A Funny Bird

Text by Béatrice Fontanel
Photos by André Fatras and Yves Cherel

READER'S DIGEST
Animal Close-Ups

This edition is published by Reader's Digest Young Families, Inc.
Pleasantville, NY 10570
www.readersdigest.com

Copyright © Éditions Milan 1989. Toulouse, France.
Original edition first published by Éditions Milan under the title *le manchot, drôle d'oiseau.*
Additional research by Sarah Rakitin

Copyright © 1992 in USA by Charlesbridge Publishing, Watertown, MA.

Cover photo copyright © 2000 Bruce Coleman, Inc./John Giustina.

Each little white spot is a penguin. They gather together to form huge colonies when it is nesting time.

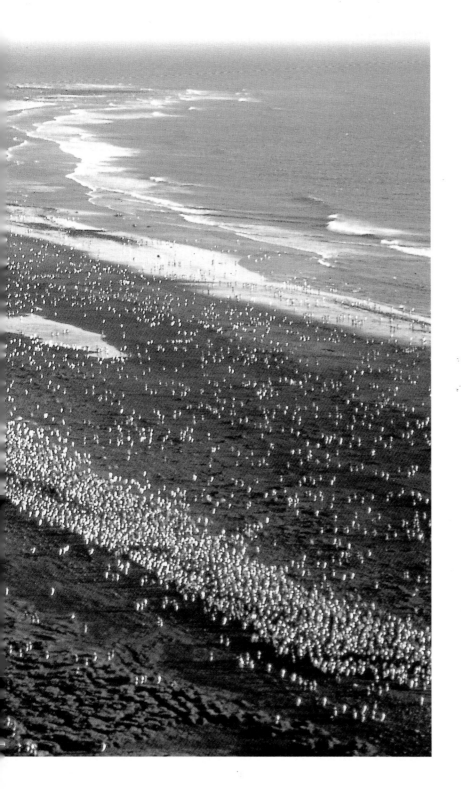

The penguin, a funny bird

At the "bottom" of the world lies a string of small rocky islands in the Antarctic ocean. Millions of king penguins live there. They cannot fly. These birds stand in the wind and rain chattering so loudly that their noise can be heard from far away.

The orange markings are very special. They help the penguins see that they are all members of the king penguin family.

Love Songs

In the southern hemisphere where the penguins live, the seasons are the opposite of ours. When summer begins in November, the penguins leave the ocean where they have been eating their fill. Grown chubby, they ride the waves and waddle across the beach to look for a mate. When penguins find their mates, they stand face to face with their beaks stretched up to the sky, and their wings back. Then they bow to each other and sing their songs.

Each penguin has its own song. In this way the male and female are able to find each other again, even though there are many thousands of pairs.

It's not easy for penguins to scratch themselves behind the head, but by bending and twisting, they can.

The largest penguin colony in the world has 300,000 couples. The birds travel to this place by following "roads" that have been worn down by penguins walking the same ways over many years.

Even though king penguins live in huge groups, they do not crowd each other. Each one keeps a small area around it, just big enough to stretch out its beak and flap its wings.

Instead of building nests, the king penguins turn their backs to the wind, and hold their eggs under them. They are very careful to keep the egg from rolling away.

In the warm penguin colony

Even in the warm season, huge storms can blow in very quickly. The penguins are well prepared to deal with storms. Their smooth bodies have a thick layer of fat under the skin, and feathers that are layered like the shingles on a roof.

No nest...
and only one egg

The female lays her egg in mid-November. It is as big as a grapefruit and pear-shaped. She places it on its side on her webbed feet! She covers it with a big fold of skin to keep it warm. This must be the strangest cradle in the world.

A few hours after laying the egg, the female penguin must go back to the ocean to eat for two or three weeks. While she is away, it is the male who takes care of the egg. He grows thinner each day. When the female returns, she takes back the precious egg and the male leaves to go eat.

When a penguin returns to take care of the egg, it bows and clicks its beak to say "I'm back. It's me. You can have your turn to fish now."

An abandoned penguin egg is a great find for an egg-eating bird like this skua.

Penguins sometimes lose their eggs after a storm or a flood.

This giant petrel will not attack a big penguin, but it will try to make a meal of a penguin egg or a baby chick.

Hurry! You must keep eating to fatten up as much as possible before the bad weather comes.

One week after birth, the baby shyly goes outside. It has no feathers and is completely helpless.

When a male or female penguin comes back from fishing, it sings its special song. Older babies recognize their parents' song and rush to them to get some food.

The chicks change their feathers

In January, the chicks hatch — knock, knock, knock. The sound of the chick trying to break through the shell goes on for two days. After it is out of the shell, the chick stays warm under its parents. A fine gray blanket of feathers begins to grow on its naked body. In three weeks, it has a thick, warm, chocolate-brown coat.

The chicks have no waterproof feathers so they cannot go fishing for food. They have to wait for their parents who go back and forth from their baby to the ocean bringing fish to feed their babies. The parents hold the fish in their throats so the baby has to reach into the parent's mouth to get the fish.

There's nothing like a nap after a good meal. This fat chick is too big to fit under its mother.

Penguins, fishers of the sea

On the islands where they live, there is nothing to eat, only rocks and a few plants. In the ocean, however, there are millions of fish, and the penguins have a feast.

The shape of a penguin's body and its waterproof feathers are perfect for swimming. They flap their wings to go forward and use their feet to steer. They look like they are flying underwater!

At swimming time, the penguins clean themselves and clown around.

Even though they spend a long time in freezing water, they do not get cold, because they have a thick layer of insulating fat and waterproof feathers.

A huge visitor shares the beach. It is an elephant seal that is 16 feet long and weighs over 3 tons. A penguin weighs only 33 pounds, so to them the elephant seal is gigantic.

To get to the water, penguins must sometimes walk through groups of elephant seals on the beach. These giants come to the land to shed their fur and to have babies. They take up a lot of space!

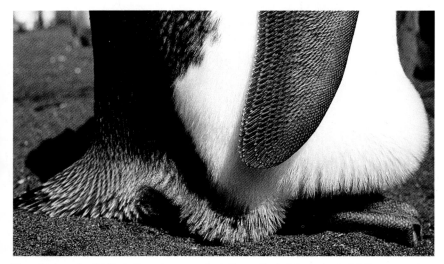

Two feet and a little tail make a perfect three-footed base to hold the penguin standing up for hours without getting tired.

When looking down at the chicks from above, the difference in their color is clear.

A hard life for a chick

A newborn chick weighs about the same as a large apple. After their parents have fed them for about four months, they weigh about 30 pounds.

In the winter the parents go off to fish, and the babies stay together on land. They squeeze together to protect themselves from the cold. Their parents return to feed them once every few weeks.

The chicks look like teddy bears except for their beaks.

The southern winter

The month of May is not easy in the southern hemisphere. Where we live it is spring and the flowers are in bloom, but where the penguins live, the terrible Antarctic winter begins.

A snow storm starts with fierce winds. The sky is gray and the land is icy. The parents who return to feed their chicks have to fight their way against the strong winds. All the penguins cooperate to keep warm.

A penguin's fat and feathers can keep its body so well insulated that the snowflakes do not melt when they land on its feathers.

To protect themselves from bad weather, they stand with their backs to the wind, forming a triangle shape. The penguins at the center often change places with the penguins at the outer edges of the triangle.

18

In gusts of wind and snow, the penguins hurry to form a warm group.

In the middle of the resting chicks, a mother calls out to her chick so she can feed it.

It looks like a penguin in disguise, but it is really a chick molting.

Holding on until the end of winter

Finally, it is September, and the weather is warmer. The full grown penguins come back from the ocean.

By October, the chubby chicks begin to lose their chocolate-brown "fur coat" as new feathers appear from underneath. This is called molting.

When the king penguin is two years old, it has an all black beak and yellow, instead of orange, markings.

Return to the colony

A year has passed. At the end of the bad weather, the grown-up penguins have returned to the colony to have babies again. Penguins have only one baby every two years, and they take very good care of it. With an average life span of twenty years, king penguin parents can have several babies.

Penguins are true sea birds. They return to the land only to have and raise their babies or to molt. Most of the time, the penguins are not on land. They are in the water with the fish. What funny birds!

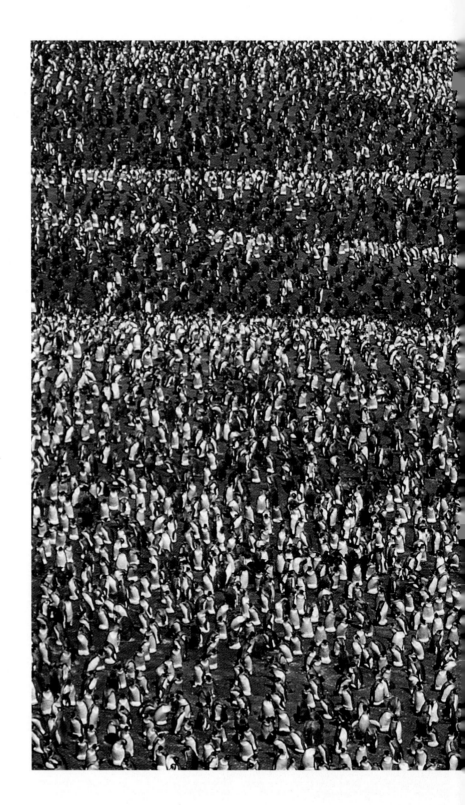

In 1620, when an explorer saw penguins for the first time, he claimed he had discovered "feathered fish"!

Once hunted

Penguins were once hunted, but are now protected by law. Their flocks grow each year. These birds have such an unusual way of life that they are a favorite subject of scientific study. However, because they live in so few areas, people are concerned about their survival.

Scientists tag penguins on their wings, unlike other birds, which are tagged on their feet.

Penguins are not afraid of people. When people are around, the penguins often follow them with curiosity.

Scientific study

There have been many scientific studies on the king penguin.

Knowing their age:
By tagging many birds, scientists have learned that the king penguin lives to be 20 years old. Some tagged penguins were found on other islands more than 620 miles from their colonies. What swimmers!

Studying their diving:
Some biologists put tiny electronic sensors on the penguins' backs to find out how many dives each one made and how deep each went. The deepest dives were about 165 feet down!

Understanding their eating habits:
Scientists are trying to understand how penguins are able to go for long periods without eating. Penguins store such large amounts of fat when they eat fish in the ocean. Then they use this supply of fat as food when they are on land for long periods of time.

Now protected

Today all types of Antarctic birds are protected. The penguin population is growing because of the ban on hunting and the abundance of food. However, we should remember that they could be wiped out if their islands became polluted.

Scientists in the Crozet Islands use helicopters to get from one penguin colony to another.

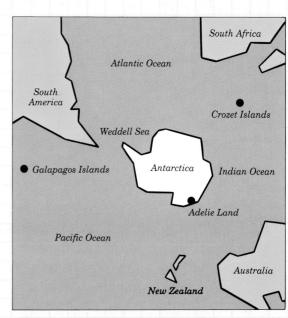

Locations where penguins live

Big and little: a family of many sizes

With rounded bodies, black backs, and white bellies, penguins all look like little gentlemen in tuxedos. They have a funny walk, but they move with great skill on ice or rocks, and when they are in the water, they are as much at home as a dolphin.

There are 17 species of penguins in the world. They all live in the Southern hemisphere.

▲
The *emperor penguin* is the biggest of the penguins. It is about three feet tall and can weigh up to 90 pounds. This bird lays its eggs on ice fields where it is so cold that only the male is able to take care of its egg until it hatches. The temperatures are -50 to -86 degrees!

The *Papuan penguin* lays its eggs among big clumps of grass. The mother lays two eggs, which will hatch out to two adorable little chicks. Papuan penguins eat a large amount of shrimp as well as fish. ▶

11   12   13   14   15   16   17

◄ The *Magellan penguins* make a nest by digging a hole with their feet and beaks. They line the hole with a carpet of grass and both sit there basking in the sun.

Rock hopper penguins have long yellow feathers on the sides of their heads. These penguins jump from rock to rock with their feet together. They make a simple nest in which they lay two eggs. The strange part is that the first egg laid is always much smaller than the second. ▶

1. Emperor penguin 2. King penguin 3. Rock hopper penguin 4. Antipodean penguin 5. Macaroni penguin 6. Royal penguin 7. Snares Island penguin 8. Crested penguin 9. Yellow eyed penguin 10. Papuan penguin 11. Chin-strap penguin 12. Adelie penguin 13. Cape penguin 14. Humbolt penguin 15. Magellan penguin 16. Galapagos penguin 17. Blue penguin

27

For Further Reading...

Arnold, Caroline. *Penguin*. Photographs by Richard Hewett. New York: Morrow Junior Books, 1988.

McMillan, Bruce. *Penguins at Home: Gentoos of Antarctica*. Photographs by Bruce McMillan. Boston: Houghton Mifflin Company, 1993.

Patent, Dorothy Hinshaw. *Looking at Penguins*. Photographs by Graham Robertson. New York: Holiday House, 1993.

To See Penguins in Captivity...

Many zoos also have web sites on the internet. To learn more about their exhibits, go to the following page on the Yahoo WWW site:

http://www.yahoo.com/science/biology/zoology/zoos

Use the Internet to Find Out More About Penguins and Their Environment...

Sea World / Busch Gardens: Penguins. Lots of information with a great index
http://www.seaworld.org/penguins/pageone.html

Zoobooks. Pet a penguin
http://www.zoobooks.com/petpp.htm

The Penguin Page. Loads of fun
http://www.vni.net/~kwelch/penguins/

Photograph credits:
DORDHAIN/FATRAS: p. 26 (top).
BIOS: Bretagnolle, p. 6-7, Thomas, p. 27
JACANA: Gohier, p. 21 (top).
CHEREL Yves: p. 7 (top right), p. 9 (top), p. 11 (top), p. 12 (bottom left), p. 15, p. 16-17, p. 21 (bottom).

© 1989 Fatras André: p. 4, p. 5, p. 8, p. 9 (bottom), p. 10, p. 11 (bottom), p. 12 (top left and right), p. 13, p. 14, p. 18-19, p. 20, p. 22-23, p. 24-25, p. 26 (bottom left).